Watery Highways

Trade and Travel in the Colonial Chesapeake

Joseph M. Greeley

HISTORIC ST. MARY'S CITY

This publication is supported in part through assistance from the National Park Service.

Cover art:
The Landing of the Maryland Colonists by Peter Egeli.
Used with permission.

Photo credits: All historical reenactments were photographed at Historic St. Mary's City, a museum of living history and archaeology on the site of Maryland's colonial capital.

Graphic design by:
Sims Design Company, LLC

Printed in the U.S. by:
HBP, Inc.

Historic St. Mary's City
P.O. Box 39
St. Mary's City, Maryland 20686
www.historicstmaryscity.museum

This book is dedicated to my father,
Samuel J.M. Greeley,
whose collection of nautical books
was a great influence on a small child,
and to my aunt and uncle,
Marghie and Forrest Watson,
who have always been a source of
unfailing help and inspiration.

Table of Contents

Historic St. Mary's City is proud to sponsor this publication, *Watery Highways: Trade and Travel in the Colonial Chesapeake.*

For decades during the seventeenth century, St. Mary's City and Jamestown were the two most fully developed towns in the Chesapeake Bay. They shipped and received goods along the Atlantic seaboard and to the Caribbean, England, and the Continent. Tobacco was the mainstay of the region's economy, and trade flourished throughout the Chesapeake's extensive network of rivers and creeks. The story of these ventures is especially meaningful to anyone who loves history and enjoys— or wishes for—a maritime way of life in the beautiful reaches of the Bay.

Joseph Greeley, interpretive supervisor for the recreated sailing vessel *Maryland Dove* and the waterfront at Historic St. Mary's City, drew upon his extensive knowledge of colonial trade, navigation, and watercraft to write the text for this publication. His enthusiasm for maritime history made this a labor of love. Susan G. Wilkinson, Marketing and Communications Director for Historic St. Mary's City, acted as project manager and dealt with the countless details of budgets, deadlines, selection of illustrations, and coordination with the book designer, Kathleen Sims. Many colleagues offered assistance at every stage of writing and production, including Dorsey Bodeman, Janet Haugaard, Silas Hurry, Dr. Henry M. Miller, Mary Ridgell, and Donald Winter.

I want to express our deep appreciation to the Chesapeake Bay Gateways Network and to its director, Jonathan Doherty, for the generous grant that has underwritten the production of *Watery Highways*. Historic St. Mary's City is honored to have been designated as a Gateways site, and we look forward to many years of continuing collaboration.

Martin Sullivan, Ph.D.
Executive Director
Historic St. Mary's City, Maryland

Foreword

Acknowledgements

A full acknowledgement of all the people who helped out would be longer than the book, but I'd like to particularly recognize the library staff at the Chesapeake Bay Maritime Museum in St. Michaels, who were very kind and helpful, and Arthur Pierce Middleton, whose seminal book *Tobacco Coast* was a source of great inspiration and information. To the rest of you, you know who you are. I couldn't have done it without you. Thank you!

Joseph M. Greeley
Waterfront Interpretive Supervisor
Historic St. Mary's City

The Chesapeake Bay

THE CHESAPEAKE BAY IS ONE OF THE NATURAL WONDERS of North America. Moreover, its presence has profoundly affected the people who settled the mid-Atlantic seaboard, from the Indians to the Europeans who followed them, to the present states of Maryland and Virginia. The Bay is an estuary, a place where the sea invades the land, and it is the largest estuary on the continent. The Chesapeake extends some 195 miles from its beginnings in the Susquehanna River to the Virginia capes where it meets the Atlantic. Its maximum width is only about 30 miles, but the tidal rivers, creeks, and inlets that corrugate its coastline form approximately 12,000 miles of shoreline. Including its tributaries, the Bay's watershed drains over 64,000 square miles, covering Virginia, Maryland, Delaware, New York, and Pennsylvania.

The Bay is not deep. Only a few places are more than 100 feet and the average depth is a mere 30 feet. Fresh and salt water meet and mingle in the Chesapeake. By the Virginia capes, where the Bay meets the Atlantic, the water is seawater. As one ascends the Bay, towards the rivers that feed into it, the water gradually freshens. Shipmasters in the 17th and 18th centuries would bring their ships as far up the rivers and streams as they could into what they called the *freshes* or fresh water to kill the shipworms that ate the hulls of their ships. Shipworms (teredo navalis, actually a burrowing mollusk) are unable to live in the low salinity levels found upstream.

The shallow depth of the Bay that allows sunlight to penetrate to the bottom, the mixing of salt and fresh water, and the broad marshlands that dot the shorelines make the Chesapeake a rich breeding ground for all manner of life.

In geologic terms, the Chesapeake Bay is of comparatively recent origin. The Bay came into existence because of the most recent Ice Age. As glaciers began creeping southward, the water locked within them was being drawn from the ocean and sea level dropped, exposing the land. The Susquehanna River, fed by ice melt from the glaciers, cut

This satellite photo of the Bay shows the extent of the watery highway available to the Indians and colonists. Photo credit: NASA GSFC, Landsat.

deep into the alluvial plain. Other rivers joined it as it flowed south to the sea, carving a wide river valley. About 10,000 years ago, when the Ice Age ended, the glaciers started retreating northwards, and as they melted, the water they contained returned to the sea. Sea level rose again and water invaded the land, filling the Susquehanna River valley and creating the Chesapeake Bay.

The incredible natural resources of the Bay made a strong impression on those who sailed its waters and enjoyed its bounty. Three centuries ago, people wrote of taking fish by the hundreds with only a baited line. Oysters were so plentiful that oyster reefs posed a hazard to navigation. Nearly every early European explorer waxed lyrical about the number and variety of fish, fowl, and animal life they saw, from enormous sturgeon to flights of birds that obscured the sun.

But rich though the Bay was, it was not merely the presence of such abundance that made the Bay so important to its inhabitants, Indian or European. Of equal importance was the fact that the Bay provided an immense watery highway for trade and travel. For over three hundred years, the Chesapeake Bay and its tributaries were not barriers to be bridged but a means of communication and commerce. Not until the 20th century and the development of automobiles and air travel did the Bay cease to be the primary means of transport for the people who lived along its shorelines.

The Chesapeake's First Citizens

HUMAN USE OF THE LANDS AND WATERS IN THE BAY region began over 12,000 years ago as nomadic hunters roamed the river valley hunting game and fishing the rivers. About 5,000 years ago, American Indians began to visit the Bay region seasonally to fish and gather oysters and crabs. Larger settlements appeared around 2,500 years ago, as the basic necessities of life—wildlife and vegetation for food, fresh water, materials for shelter and tools—could be found in abundance. By 1,000 years ago, Indians were cultivating a variety of crops, including corn and tobacco, on the rich lands surrounding the Bay.

The Indian people had a well-developed system of overland trails, but in the Chesapeake region, so heavily laced with innumerable inlets, rivers, marshes and streams, travel by land meant taking long, round-about routes. It was easier and quicker to cross the water, and the common means of transport was the dugout canoe. In the Americas, dugout canoes have been used for thousands of years. The oldest known example, found in Florida, is dated at about 5,000 years old, and a pictograph depicting a dugout found in Texas may be as old as 8,000 years.

The American Indians of the Chesapeake constructed everything from small one-man canoes to huge dugouts, 40 to 50 feet in length, capable of carrying two dozen people. Log canoes served many purposes. Larger canoes could be used for making war, transporting large numbers of people, or moving cargo. Smaller canoes were used to cross relatively narrow bodies of water and for harvesting fish and shellfish, an important part of the American Indian diet and a source of materials for tools. Some fishing was done by wading in the shallows to gather oysters or spear fish, but the American Indians also built fish traps, or weirs, that directed the fish into an enclosure from which the fish could be scooped into canoes using nets.

The Manner of Makinge Theyre Boates *illustrates Chesapeake Indians' use of fire and shells to scrape out their dugout canoes. Theodor De Bry, an engraver and book maker from Frankfurt, produced some of the earliest images of the New World. He based the engravings on paintings by John White, who led a 16th-century expedition to what is now North Carolina.*

Waterways made it easier to carry large amounts of trade goods, even allowing for short portages from one channel to another. Thus most trade was carried out using water routes. Archaeological and historical evidence indicate that the American Indians had extensive trade routes. It was possible for American Indians to travel from the Chesapeake to the Ohio River Valley along rivers. Copper from the Great Lakes region, where it occurred as nuggets of ore, was one of the most highly prized trade items, as were certain stones. Rhyolite was in great demand for tool making. This stone, found in Western Maryland, was traded down the Potomac over 1,500 years ago. While luxury goods such as copper and shells for ornamentation and stone for tools, formed the basis for most long distance trade, there may also have been some local trade in foodstuffs.

Water also served as a pathway for enemies. When the colonists who settled Maryland arrived in 1634, they found the native Yaocomaco people being raided by the Susquehannock from farther north. The Susquehannock used birch-bark canoes that were lighter and faster than the Yaocomaco dugouts. This made it difficult for the Yaocomaco to retaliate effectively, and they were in the process of moving farther south to avoid the raids when the English arrived. The Yaocomaco may have welcomed the English because they saw that the colonists, with their ships and weapons, could serve as an effective barrier between them and their enemies. Good relations with the American Indians was one reason the fourth permanent colony in English North America was a success.

John White's painting Their manner of fishynge in Virginia *shows the dugout canoes and fishing weirs used by the American Indians.*

"... ther was never seene among us so cunninge a way to take fish withall ..." observed Thomas Harriot, mathematician, navigator, and member of the 1586 expedition to today's North Carolina.

A Ship to Master the Oceans

EUROPEAN AWARENESS OF THE BAY BEGAN IN THE 16TH century when explorers looking for the fabled Northwest Passage, the legendary shortcut from the Atlantic to the Pacific, discovered what seemed like a promising prospect halfway up the North American seaboard. This was the Chesapeake Bay. As early as 1527, official Spanish maps showed the Chesapeake Bay as the Bahia de Santa Maria (St. Mary's Bay). The Spanish, attempting to maintain their claim to all of the Americas, made regular forays up the coast from their holdings in Florida. In the 1570s, they attempted to establish a mission in the Chesapeake but were driven away by the Indians.

The arrival of Europeans in the Bay, and the colonization and trade that followed the voyages of discovery, were possible only because of a revolution in ship design and improvement in navigational techniques that occurred in the 15th and 16th centuries. In 1400, there were few European ships capable of making an Atlantic voyage once, let alone repeatedly. Navigation was in its infancy and consisted mainly of the use of landmarks to grope one's way along a coastline. Two things spurred this revolution. The first was increased contact between Northern Europe and the Mediterranean, the second was the advance of Islam. When Constantinople fell to the Turks in 1453 it sent shockwaves through Europe. Not only was a major bastion of Christianity in the Middle East now gone, but Muslims now controlled the route through which the spices of the Far East flowed to European markets. It was imperative that another route to the Indies be found. The only two possible routes were southwards around Africa or out across the Western Ocean. Both would require a tough maneuverable ship capable of making long voyages.

The ships that crossed the Atlantic to the Americas and to the Chesapeake were a melding of traditions from Northern Europe and from the Mediterranean. Northern European shipbuilders, including the builders of Viking longships, used clinker construction where planks overlap. While sturdy and flexible, there are size limitations to clinker construction. Mediterranean shipwrights on the other hand, used what would become called caravel construction where planks are set edge to edge. Caravel built ships can be built larger and stronger, better able to weather conditions on the open ocean.

Both Northern European and Mediterranean ships were originally steered with side rudders, but in the 1200s shipwrights in the North developed the stern rudder. The stern rudder was both easier to control and more efficient than steering oars.

Above left: *This photograph of the* Maryland Dove *under construction shows the frame-first method of ship construction.*

Above: *On the right, clinker planking was used in Northern Europe from the Dark Ages. The Vikings followed the islands of the Northern Atlantic to Labrador in this type of boat. On the left, Mediterranean-style caravel planking was adopted by the 15th century.*

Opposite: *This stern shot of the* Maryland Dove *shows the stern rudder, which began replacing the steering oar in the 12th century.*

The lateen, or Latin, sail was introduced into the Mediterranean by Arab seafarers. The lateen sail allowed ships to sail closer to the wind than a square sail.

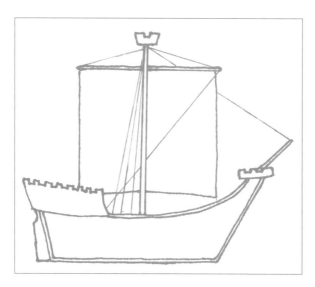

The square sail, while not as efficient when sailing close to the wind as a fore and aft sail like the lateen sail, was more efficient when sailing before the wind.

The square sail (so called not because of its shape, but because it is set at a 90 degree angle to the axis of the ship) was used by both Northern Europe and the Mediterranean from ancient times until the Dark Ages, when it was superseded in the Mediterranean by the lateen sail. The lateen is a fore and aft sail, meaning that it runs along the axis of the ship, rather than across it. A fore and aft rigged ship can sail closer to the wind than a ship rigged with a square sail, which suited conditions in the Mediterranean excellently. Crossing the Atlantic however, required a ship that had both types of sails.

By the 1470s such a ship had appeared. It used caravel construction, had a stern rudder and carried square sails on the main and fore masts to drive the ship. The mizzen (rearmost) mast had a lateen sail which helped balance the ship to aid in steering. A small square sail called a spritsail was set on a long pole or bowsprit off the front of the vessel which also aided in balancing the ship. From Columbus's voyages until the end of the age of sail, some variation of this rig could be seen on almost all large sailing ships. Those who came to the Chesapeake in the 17th and 18th centuries traveled on this type of ship.

This print of 16th-century Dutch vessels shows the combination rig developed in Northern Europe with a lateen sail on the mizzen and square sails on the main and fore masts.

In the Mediterranean, dual steering oars remained in use longer due to the difficulty of fitting a rudder to the curved sternpost. Complete Book of Maritime Design.

The steering oar gave rise to the modern sailor's terms for right and left. Since the oar was mounted on the right because the majority of people are right handed, the right was referred to as the steering board or "starboard" side. The left side of the ship was the side that was used for loading the ship, since the ship was canted to the left when beached to avoid damage to the steering oar. Hence the left side was referred as the loading board or "larboard" side. In the late 18th century, "larboard" was replaced by "port" since in high winds it was easy to confuse the words starboard and larboard.

The Haven-Finding Art

A SHIP THAT CAN CROSS 3,000 MILES AND MORE OF OCEAN is of little use if future travelers cannot find their way to the same spot. The techniques that mariners used in the 16th and 17th centuries, while far from exact, enabled them to make landfall with reasonable accuracy. Navigation, however, was a skill usually restricted to the officers. Common sailors could steer a course and determine the ships' speed but had no idea how to determine latitude or longitude.

Navigation has its origins in pilotage, the art of coastal sailing. Until the mid-15th century, all navigation was pilotage—and ships rarely ventured out of sight of land. Pilotage involved a thorough knowledge of the coast, including landmarks, compass bearings, tides, water depths, and bottom type in the area the ship was sailing. Even today, the pilots who guide ships in and out of harbors around the world are required to have an exhaustive knowledge of the waters they traverse. In the 15th and 16th centuries, shipmasters composed *rutters,* books of sailing directions giving all these details. Early on, these were usually hand-written for the master's own use, but by the 17th century, *rutters* were being published and sold throughout Europe. Still, a ship's master would have had a difficult time navigating unfamiliar creeks, coves, shoals and spits using drawings and directions of the Chesapeake Bay.

Soon after the British arrived in the region, professional pilots became available to guide ships through the Chesapeake's waters. The Virginia colony quickly began regulating and licensing pilots, but during the first years of the Maryland colony, anyone who chose could serve as a pilot and charge what traffic would bear. Competition kept rates down, and reputation kept the incompetent from causing too much trouble. Still, court records describe many voyages gone wrong—boats grounded, ports missed, and merchants and pilots battling for damages or pay.

The term *rutter* is derived from the French *routier,* a ship route chart.

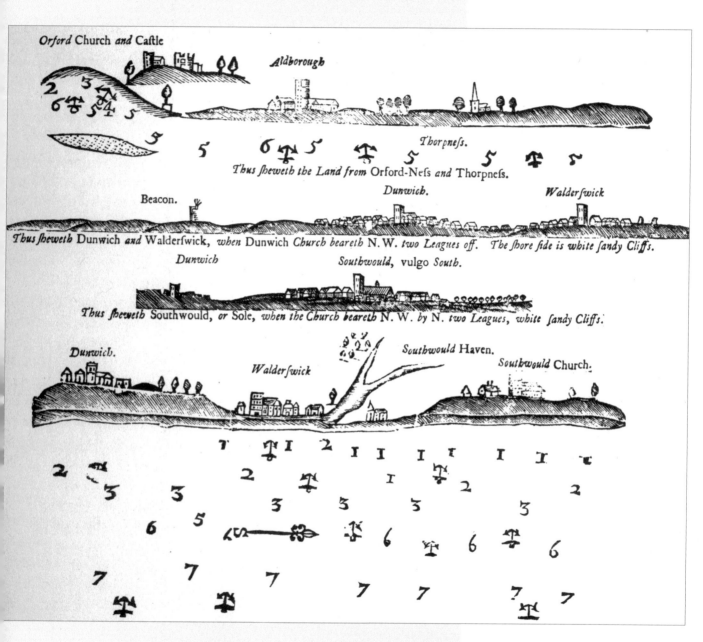

Orford Church *and* Castle

Aldborough

Thorpness.

Thus sheweth the Land from Orford-Ness and Thorpness.

Beacon.

Dunwich.

Walderswick

Thus sheweth Dunwich *and* Walderswick, *when Dunwich Church beareth N.W. two Leagues off. The shore side is white sandy Cliffs.*

Dunwich

Southwould, *vulgo South.*

Thus sheweth Southwould, *or Sole, when the Church beareth N.W. by N. two Leagues, white sandy Cliffs.*

Dunwich.

Walderswick

Southwould Haven.

Southwould Church.

This page from a Rutter *shows landmarks, water depths, and anchorages, the sort of navigational aids used by mariners in the period.*

The Tools of the Navigator

SAILING OUT OF SIGHT OF LAND REQUIRED ANOTHER SET OF skills. The Portuguese were the first Europeans to develop this ability. In the 1400s, the Portuguese were making longer and longer voyages to Africa and discovered that the best way to reach the Ivory and Gold Coasts was to follow the winds out of sight of land and then back again to landfall on the African coast. The Spanish learned from the Portuguese when the two kingdoms were joined in the late 1500s. This knowledge enabled Spain to establish her overseas empire, and the riches that Spain found in the New World inspired other European nations to seek their share.

Knowledge of deep-sea navigation flowered in England during the course of the 16th century. In 1500, eight years after Columbus's first voyage, there was not a single seaman in England capable of duplicating his effort. But by the end of the 16th century, English seamen and navigators were considered some of the best in the world, and by the end of the 17th century, the English had contact and trade with every part of the globe.

In the 17th century, no truly accurate method existed for measuring longitude at sea (the distance east or west). Surveyors on land could compute longitude by observing celestial phenomena, such as eclipses, but these methods required the observer to remain still for a long period of time, something that was impossible on the deck of a ship. Instead, navigators relied on a method called dead reckoning, possibly a shortening of deduced reckoning. The main instruments for determining dead reckoning were the compass, the log line, and the traverse board, used along with the half-hour sandglass, to track the watches, and a 28-second sandglass used to time the log line.

*A school of navigation, from a
17th-century book of navigation.*

The compass was developed in China and introduced to Europe by Marco Polo in the 12th century. An early compass was simply a magnetized iron needle balanced on a piece of wood that was floating in a bowl of water. The free moving needle aligns with the earth's magnetic field, one end pointing north.

The log line was used to figure the ship's speed. A piece of wood, called a *chip,* was attached to a line on a reel. A white rag was tied into the line at 90 feet. From that point the line was knotted at intervals of 47 feet 3 inches, the equivalent of 1/128 of a nautical mile. The chip was tossed overboard where it would float relatively still while the ship sailed away from it. The first 90 feet of line off the reel allowed the chip to float clear of any turbulence from the wake of the ship. As this length, marked by the rag, passed over the stern of the ship, a 28-second sandglass was started. When the sand had run through the glass, the line was stopped. Since the 28-second hourglass measures 1/128th of an hour and the knots on the line represent 1/128th of a nautical mile, the number of marks that had run out corresponded to the ship's speed in nautical miles an hour, or knots. The log was run every two hours unless a change of wind caused the ship's speed to increase or decrease markedly.

The compass rose described direction using 32 points. Between north and east are north by east, north northeast, northeast by north, north east, northeast by east, east northeast, and east by north.

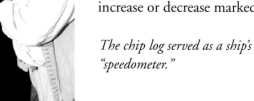

The chip log served as a ship's "speedometer."

The most common error with the log line was a miscalculation of speed, since currents can give a false reading on the chip log. For example, if the ship is making five knots through the water, but is running against a two-knot current, the actual distance covered each hour is only three nautical miles.

The speed was recorded using a peg on a traverse board. The top of the traverse board had a compass rose marked on it and eight concentric rings of holes radiating out from the center, each line of holes corresponding to one of the 32 compass points. Every half hour, the course being steered was marked on the appropriate hole, starting at the center and working outwards. Thus, at the end of a four-hour watch, the traverse board held a complete record of course and speed for the last four hours. This would be duly recorded in the logbook by the deck officer, then the traverse board would be cleared for the next watch.

The navigator could then take those readings and calculate longitude, or direction east and west, based on how far the ship had traveled that day. Although prone to error, dead reckoning was used throughout the 17th and 18th centuries until the introduction of John Harrison's marine clock in the 1780s.

The traverse board was used to record speed and direction to help the navigator determine distance traveled east or west longitude.

Latitude, or the distance north and south, could be computed with a fair degree of accuracy, using the sun or Polaris, the North Star. A number of instruments were available to the 17th-century navigator for measuring latitude. The oldest and simplest is the quadrant, a quarter of a circle with a plumb bob affixed to the apex and degrees marked along the curved edge. By sighting the sun or North Star through sights along the top, reading the number of degrees cut by the string, and performing a few mathematical calculations, the navigator got his latitude. A related instrument is the astrolabe, a full circle with a pivoting arm and sight vanes mounted on the arm. Using these instruments on the deck of a rolling ship made them relatively inaccurate. Even a good navigator would be hard pressed to find his latitude with accuracy

The quadrant was one of the earliest navigational devices used to determine latitude by sighting sun or stars. It was also one of the least accurate.

greater than one degree, or 60 nautical miles, but that was often sufficient to make landfall. In making a long ocean crossing, a 17th-century navigator would sail to the latitude where the easiest passage could be made and then sail along that latitude until land was sighted. From there, a position could be established using landmarks, and the ship could sail along the coast to reach its final destination.

As the 17th century progressed, devices for measuring latitude were refined. The cross staff was more accurate than the quadrant, but not any easier to use, especially as it required the observer to stare directly at the sun for long periods with resulting damage to his eyes. The back staff or Davis quadrant was a significant improvement on the cross staff. It consisted of two semi-arcs attached to a frame. On the larger arc was the sight vane, on the smaller was the shadow vane. A horizon vane with a slot for viewing the horizon was placed on the end of the staff below the shadow arc. The navigator stood with his back to the sun and peered through the sight vane and horizon vane, then adjusted the sight vane and shadow

The astrolabe, cross staff, and backstaff were all used by navigators in the 17th century. The backstaff was the most accurate, least damaging to one's eyesight, and the most expensive.

vane until the shadow line from the shadow vane lay across the horizon vane. The navigator then read from the shadow arc and the sighting arc and added the figures together to get the sun's altitude. Because it relied on a shadow, the Davis quadrant could not be used to take a star sight, but in the hands of a good navigator, it could fix latitude to within 10–15 nautical miles.

The lead line may have been the most useful tool in the 17th-century navigator's arsenal. It consisted of nothing more than a weight attached to a length of rope. A hole in the bottom of the lead was filled with tallow, then the lead line would be thrown overboard and allowed to sink until it touched something solid. In this way, the leadsman brought up a sample of the bottom. Charts were marked with water depths and the type of bottom, a feature that can still be seen on modern charts. An experienced navigator could often tell his position by the use of the lead line alone. Off the Virginia coastline, out of sight of land but within "soundings" (the depth where the line could reach bottom) the bottom sample that the lead brought up told the navigator if he was off the mouth of the Bay. At the entrance, the bottom is mud and sand mixed with white shell. Above and below the capes that mark the entrance, the bottom is reddish-colored, hard-packed sand. Navigators could, to a certain extent, follow the contours of the bottom, turning towards shore when the water became too deep to measure with the lead line and turning out to sea when the water began to shallow.

Using the lead line, a skilled navigator could tell the water's depth but also, in some cases, where he was.

Although the methods of 16th- and 17th-century navigators may seem primitive to modern eyes, they should not be underrated. Without these tools and techniques, the exploration and settlement of the Chesapeake Bay by Europeans would not have been possible.

The English and the Chesapeake

THE ENGLISH, INTENT ON GAINING A FOOTHOLD IN THE New World, became the first to establish a permanent settlement in the Chesapeake region after two failed attempts to settle in the region that is now North Carolina. In 1607, the *Susan Constant,* the *Godspeed,* and the *Discovery* sailed under the auspices of the Virginia Company. They carried their cargo of English colonists and supplies up the Chesapeake to the James River. There, on the northern shore, where the water was deep enough to moor the ships to trees on the shoreline, they established Jamestown (Virginia), which became the first permanent English colony in North America.

The English efforts at colonization were initially driven by hopes of finding the same riches in North America as the Spanish had found in South and Central America, and by the hope of finding the fabled Northwest Passage. The Northwest Passage was sought as a way of avoiding the long and dangerous voyage through the Spanish controlled Straights of Magellan (or later around Cape Horn) or the equally long and dangerous route around the Cape of Good Hope (the southern tip of Africa). A more direct route to the East Indies would help the English break the Portuguese monopoly on the lucrative spice trade. Alas for the English, the Chesapeake failed to provide access to the Pacific, or large deposits of gold and silver, but its abundant natural resources, and the watery highway it provided to its inhabitants were, in the long run, equally advantageous.

Map by Flemish scholar, geographer, and one of the most prominent geographers of the sixteenth century, Abraham Ortelius, from the revolutionary mapbook Theatrum Orbis Terrarum.

Another 1607 English expedition sent out by the rival Plymouth-based Virginia Company settled the Popham colony on the Kennebec River in present day Maine at the same time, but was abandoned because of the severe winters there.

Shortly after the establishment of Jamestown, the colonists began to explore their new home. Captain John Smith led the first expeditions to explore the Bay and its tributaries—the Potomac, the Susquehanna, the Patuxent, and Rappahannock Rivers. During his travels, Smith met up with Powhatan Indians, from whom he learned the names of many of the rivers and places he mapped. The map produced by Smith was remarkably accurate, and many of the place names are still in use today.

Smith was greatly impressed by the sights he saw in his travels. He wrote that around the Chesapeake Bay: *"... is a country that may have the prerogative over the most pleasant places of Europe, Asia, Africa, or America for large and pleasant navigable rivers, heaven and earth never agreed better to frame a place for mans habitation."* Smith was not a wholly disinterested observer, since he was writing to attract settlers to the Virginia colony, but we know from other accounts and from historical evidence that if he exaggerated the natural wonders of the Bay it was not by much.

Jacques le Moyne de Morgues, 16th-century French artist, cartographer, and explorer, illustrated early expeditions to the New World.

Map of Virginia drawn by Captain John Smith.

The early years of the Jamestown settlement were brutal. The colonists had to adjust to new foods, a new climate, new diseases, and new ways to make a living. Despite the challenges, more men and women came to the colony and new families were formed, ensuring that people stayed in the area. By 1619, Jamestown was firmly established as the seat of government, a new economy was emerging, and other settlements were springing up. By 1631, Virginia traders had established outposts as far north as Kent Island on Maryland's Eastern Shore.

In 1634, a second English colony was planted in the Bay. A group of gentlemen investors, led by Cecilius Calvert, second Lord Baltimore sponsored the new settlement on lands granted to Calvert as Lord Proprietor by King Charles I. A hired ship named the *Ark* carried approximately 140 colonists plus their equipment and supplies across the Atlantic to the Bay.

The instructions given to those planning their trip to Maryland suggested they bring goods that would enable them to take advantage of the tidewater location of the colony. These included, *"Provisions for Fishing and Fowling. Inprimis, necessaries for a boate of 3. or 4. Tunne; as Spikes, Nayles, Pitch, Tarre, Ocome, Canvis for a sayle, ropes, Anchor, Iron for the Ruther: Fishinglines for Cod and Macrills, etc. Cod-hookes, and Macrill-hookes, a Seane of Basse-net, Herringnetts, Leade, Fowling-pieces of six foote; Powder and Shott, and Flint Stones; a good Water-Spaniell, etc."*

The *Ark* was accompanied by a much smaller ship, named the *Dove*, which was purchased in England by Leonard Calvert and some of the investors to serve the colony as a trading ship after the *Ark* returned to England. The ships arrived at the end of February and, after a short stay at Point Comfort in Virginia, proceeded up the Bay to the Potomac River.

Father Andrew White, an English Jesuit and one of Maryland's original colonists, wrote the only account of the voyage to Maryland. *". . . Chesapeake Bay flows gently between the shores . . . teeming with fish . . . I have never seen a greater or more delightful river [the Potomac]; compared to it the Thames seems a mere rivulet. It is not tainted by swamps, but on both sides wonderful forests of fine trees rise up on solid ground . . . the soil seems especially fertile. . . we tread on strawberries, vines, sassafras, acorns, and nuts . . . . An abundance of springs supplies drink. No other mammals appear besides deer, beaver, and squirrels, which compare in size to European hares. Infinite is the number of birds*

Cecil Calvert, 2nd Lord Baltimore and the first Lord Proprietor of Maryland.

The Yaocomaco, who had never seen a ship as large as those the Maryland colonists arrived in, sent messengers who reported ". . . a Canoe, like an island had come with as many men as there were trees in the woods," stated Father Andrew White's in *Chronicle of the Journey to Maryland.*

of various colors, such as eagles, herons, swans, geese, partridges, and ducks. On account of this one can infer that this region does not lack the sort of things that serve the convenience and pleasure of its inhabitants."

In early March 1634, the voyagers established a camp on St. Clement's Island in the Potomac River. Although St. Clement's, named for the martyr who was thrown into the sea with an anchor roped around his neck, was defensible, it was too small to establish a permanent settlement. Cecilius' brother, Leonard Calvert, explored the river and entered into negotiations with the Yaocomaco Indians, who inhabited the lower Potomac, to purchase their village and surrounding land. Governor Calvert led the colonists back down the Potomac River about fifteen miles to the mouth of a river they named for St. George, the patron saint of England. This river came to be known as the St. Mary's, for the city the colonists established along its banks.

When the English arrived at what would become St. Mary's City, the Yaocomaco were in the process of abandoning their village because of attacks by the Susquehannock who lived further north. The inhabitants may have been happy to have the English, with their superior weapons, as a buffer between them and the more warlike Susquehannock.

They gave the colonists the benefit of already constructed shelters. Some of the natives stayed until their crops were harvested and taught the English about growing and cooking corn and their new environ-

First Landing of Leonard Calvert in Maryland *shows Father Andrew White, an English Jesuit who accompanied the colonists to Maryland, encountering the American Indians.*
ca. 1865–70, by David Acheson Woodward by permission The Maryland Historical Society, Baltimore, MD.

ment. These advantages, along with the lessons learned from earlier English settlements, helped Lord Baltimore's party avoid the difficulties suffered by earlier colonies. In fact, the new Maryland colony was actually able to export surplus corn to New England in the fall of their first year.

The most unusual aspect of the new colony of Maryland was that the Calverts and many of the gentlemen investors were Catholics at a time when the officially sanctioned church in England was Anglican. However, Maryland was not founded as a refuge for English Catholics. The bulk of the colonists aboard the *Ark* were Protestants, as were the majority of the emigrants thereafter. Although it is difficult to pinpoint the motives of people who have been dead for 300 years or more, it seems clear that the intent of most people who came to Maryland, Protestant or Catholic, was to make their fortunes. For the small number of Catholics, the freedom from tithes to the Anglican Church, and the ability to vote and hold office, while these rights lasted, was an important factor as well.

For the first few months of the Maryland colony, the settlers inhabited the witchotts left by the American Indians.

Leonard Calvert and later governors encouraged settlement on the townlands of St. Mary's City, which was established as capital of the colony. However, the tobacco economy that emerged kept settlers spread out on plantations and prevented St. Mary's from becoming the bustling city the Calverts had envisioned. Although the population was relatively small, there were many visitors who came to the capital to conduct business with the government and to trade goods. When political and religious upheaval prompted removal of the capital to Annapolis in 1695, the city's main reason for existence vanished and, shortly thereafter, so did the city. Within 50 years nearly all trace of the former first city of Maryland had disappeared.

New Worlders

CARVING A NEW COLONY OUT OF THE WILDERNESS required enormous amounts of labor. The Chesapeake colonies' leaders found workers among those suffering from the poor economic conditions and rigid class system in England. Men, and some women and children, signed an agreement, an indenture, to work in exchange for transportation to the colony, food, clothing, and shelter once they arrived. An indenture typically bound an adult servant for four or five years and children until they reached the age of majority. Those who survived their term received freedom dues that usually included a new suit of clothes, an axe, two hoes, three barrels of corn, and the rights to fifty acres of land. The servants were able to claim this land once they raised funds to have it surveyed and patented, or recorded—no small task for a newly freed indenture.

To many poor youths in England in the 17th century, an indenture seemed like a golden opportunity. The chance to own their own land, something they could never hope to achieve in England, made the risks of the journey seem worthwhile. Once they were aboard ship though, it may have seemed like less of a bargain.

A trip across the Atlantic involved at least three weeks and sometimes over two months without sight of land. Social distinctions, so important in England, were brought aboard with the passengers, so to some extent the rigors of an ocean voyage depended on who you were. Lower-ranking passengers were normally kept in the 'tween deck of a ship. The space was confining and probably quite crowded, not only with people, but supplies and cargo as well. Passengers of lesser rank were not normally allowed on deck except at certain times of the day so that they would not get in the way of the sailors working the ship.

The food was the same day after day: beans and salt beef or pork that was often half rotten or so long in the cask that it resembled rock more than meat. The only ventilation came from the main cargo hatch and the smaller hatches that were used for access. In fair weather these were

An indenture form like this would have set out the terms of a servant's contract.

This Indenture made the   Day of
in the Colony of Maryland   of the one
Party   of the County and Hundred aforefaid
of the other party,   whittnesseth that the faid
          for and in confideration of
Pounds of Tobacco paid unto and for the ufe of the faid by
the aforefaid   whittnesseth that the faid
for and in confideration of the Somme of Tobbaco aforefaid,
doth by thefe Present Covenent Bargain and Bind Himfelf for
to fearve the forefaid   and his Heirs
Executors and Adminiftrators and Affignes   from
the day of the date hereof.

The Wm Nuthead Prefs
Sainte Maries Citty, Maryland,

The English weren't the only people who came to the colonies. Records show that two individuals described as mulattos, individuals of mixed race—usually African and other parentage traveled with Maryland's first colonists as servants. The Jesuits claimed a headright for a man named Fernando, who later disappeared from the records. Matthias de Sousa also served the Jesuits, was freed by 1641, and found work as a mariner and fur trader. The next year, de Sousa participated in the assembly as a freeman and was the first man of African descent to vote in colonial America. Shortly thereafter he disappeared from the records, either dying or moving away. The first known blacks in Virginia arrived in 1619. They probably were indentured servants.

Mathias Soufa a Molato

opened or covered with gratings that allowed air to circulate. In foul weather they were sealed tightly to prevent water from entering. Diseases such as typhoid or dysentery often spread rapidly. Even in fair weather the stench from seasick landsmen crowded together in tight quarters must have been appalling. One of the nicknames sailors had for landsmen in the era was *pukestockings*. High status or low, all shared in the risks of an ocean voyage—pirates and enemy warships, storms and shipwrecks, disease and accidents—and the grinding boredom and monotony of day after day on the rolling sea. The first signs of land—organic matter, plants, logs, branches in the water, land birds, the smell of pine forests, and water changing from the deep blue of mid-ocean to offshore green—must have been most welcome.

Through the 1600s, most of the immigrants to the Chesapeake region were young, white, male, indentured servants. Many did not survive the diseases they encountered in the new environment and those that did survive had shorter life spans. There were also many more men than women. Servants could not marry until the end of their indenture, unless the binding contract could be bought out. Consequently, women married later and had fewer children and it was less likely for a male settler to find a wife. Because of these difficulties it would not be until the end of the 17th century that native-born colonists began to outnumber immigrants. Meanwhile, the American Indian population was decimated by continued warfare with neighboring tribes, the introduction of European diseases, and displacement by English immigrants.

Of all the hazards faced by the sailors and passengers who came to the Chesapeake, the most common was the grinding monotony of an empty sea and sky day after day.

In the New World, luck and hard work could bring good fortune.

Expansion

The Virginia colonists' early hopes of finding gold and silver, as Spain had done in Central and South America, soon faded. In 1612, John Rolfe planted tobacco seeds brought from the Oronoco region of South America in Jamestown, and the colonists discovered that growing tobacco was almost as good as striking gold.

Christopher Columbus is credited with introducing tobacco to Europe following his explorations of the Americas. Through the 16th century, other explorers and travelers spread tobacco throughout the continent. By the first decades of the 17th century, tobacco had become one of England's most popular imports. The Spaniards' success in establishing tobacco plantations in Haiti and Cuba led to their efforts to control the tobacco market. English settlers began competing with the Spanish monopoly. By 1614, they were able to grow enough tobacco to ship to England. From that point, production expanded rapidly.

The presence of the Chesapeake Bay significantly affected the evolution of both Virginia and Maryland as tobacco-producing colonies. The Bay made it easy to transport people and goods, including heavy hogsheads of tobacco. Moving tobacco by land was expensive, difficult, and usually resulted in damaged, and less profitable, tobacco. Producing tobacco close to the shore meant planters could load their product onto a ship directly or after a short overland trip.

Early settlement in the colonies followed the water's edge. Creek shores, where weather was somewhat moderated, was claimed first, followed by the land on the river and the Bay. Access to waterways meant access to the world, since travel by water was the only practical way to move

Tobacco was initially hailed as a remedy for toothache, falling fingernails, worms, halitosis, lockjaw, bubonic plague, migraines, labor pains, asthma, cancer, and other maladies, including lung diseases. Smoking for pleasure, or to satisfy an addiction, quickly followed.

about the Chesapeake in the early days of settlement. The water's edge offered other advantages to planters. Ownership of some high and some low land followed traditional farming practices in England. A farmer who controlled some low and wet land and some high and well-drained land would be more likely to have success with his crops and livestock whether the weather was wet or dry.

Tobacco rapidly exhausts the soil in which it is grown. The "vile sotweed" could be grown on a plot of land for about three to five years before the soil was too depleted to give a profitable crop. The land then was used for corn for two or three years. Afterward it had to lie fallow for twenty years before tobacco could be profitably grown on it again. It was necessary for the planter to frequently shift the area in which tobacco was planted. This is a key reason settlement in the Chesapeake region was widespread instead of concentrated in towns, as in New England. It was not until the 1740s, when the Inspection Acts were passed, that towns truly began to thrive. These laws required that tobacco be brought to a warehouse in a designated location, such as Annapolis, for inspection before shipment to England.

In Maryland, twenty years after the first settlers arrived, Lord Baltimore was forced to begin placing limits on the amount of waterfront land that could be taken. It was important to keep some of the most appealing areas available to attract future colonists. Settlement of the interior didn't begin until late in the 17th century, when waterfront land was no longer available.

Excerpt from a 17th-century map drawn by Augustine Herrman. The plantations he noted on this 1670 document have been colored red to clearly show settlement along the edges of the watery highways.

The Tobacco Trade

MORE THAN ANY OF THE ENGLISH COLONIES IN NORTH America, Virginia and Maryland depended on maritime trade. This was both a cause and a result of their dependence on tobacco as their staple crop.

Because labor in the Chesapeake was relatively scarce and expensive and tobacco profits relatively high, it was more economical to raise tobacco to trade for goods rather than to make them. England, like Spain, France, Holland, and other colonial powers, viewed its colonies as a source of raw materials. Colonies provided the motherland with necessities they would otherwise import from other nations. The colonies were also viewed as ready-made markets for the products of the home country. Large-scale manufacturing in the colonies was discouraged and, in some cases, forbidden by law. Following this rule, beaver pelts trapped in Virginia were exported to England, processed into felt, made into hats, and exported back to the colonies for sale, and so on.

Tobacco was so profitable that laws were passed in Virginia and Maryland to ensure that tobacco farmers also raised enough corn to feed themselves, their families, and their servants. Thus the colonists relied on trans-Atlantic trade and exchange with other colonies for clothing, furniture, tools, wine, flour, salt, and spices, nearly all the necessities of life except basic foodstuffs. Because of a shortage of coinage, tobacco became the monetary standard.

Some entrepreneurial shipmasters acted as agents for tobacco planters, taking tobacco on consignment and using the profits to purchase goods in England. Sometimes shipmasters arranged inden-

It was more economical to raise tobacco to trade for goods rather than to make them.

tures, transporting individuals to the Americas, and then selling the contract in the colony. Because they transported workers into the colony, they often received a headright, or land grant. In the early years of the colony, headrights ranged from 50–200 acres. Generally an indenture was a good investment, and some shipmasters became quite wealthy.

Occasionally a wealthy merchant or shipmaster owned ocean-faring vessels, but most merchant ships were owned on the share system. Ownership of a vessel ensured that cargo space would be available when it was needed. A merchant, rather than putting all his money into one vessel, would buy shares in several so that if one ship was lost, he would not lose his whole investment. Profits from the voyage were divided among the investors according to the number of shares held. The shipmaster might be hired by the investors, or he might own shares in his ship. Crew, on the other hand, were normally hired for the duration of a voyage and paid off on the ship's return, after which they were free to sign on again or seek another ship.

A fortunate shipmaster might own a ship.

"That every person inhabitant of this colony planting tobacco shall yearly at the season plant and tend or cause to be planted and tended two acres of corn for his own food . . ."

Doing Business with Other Nations

Although most of the Chesapeake colonies' trade was with England, there were other traders present through the 17th century. In the early 17th century, Holland dominated the carrying trade. Dutch vessels traded everywhere, to the farthest reaches of the globe. The Dutch East India Company was the most powerful of the merchant trading companies, surpassing its rival, the English East India Company.

To the English settlers of the Chesapeake, the Dutch traders provided an additional market for their tobacco and a source of European goods that English merchants could not, or would not, provide. Dutch traders were especially important to the Chesapeake during the political upheavals of the English Civil War and the turbulent years that followed.

Starting in the mid-17th century, however, the English government passed a series of laws known collectively as the Navigation Acts. These laws were intended to boost the British economy by forbidding the colonies to trade certain goods, including tobacco, with any country except Great Britain. The law required that goods be shipped in vessels owned by English citizens and operated by crews that were mostly Englishmen. Goods could be shipped only to other English colonies or to ports in England itself. For example, the Oronoco tobacco grown in Maryland had to shipped to England and a duty paid before it was re-exported to Europe.

Enforcement of the Acts was an unrelenting problem for the Chesapeake colonies. In the early years, Maryland's leadership was chastised by the King for their negligence. Still, colonial court records describe numerous suits against violators.

The Navigation Acts had several, mostly unintended, results. As hoped, Dutch traders became scarcer in the Chesapeake. Another result was a dramatic increase in smuggling. Finally, in 1667 and 1673, Dutch warships sent to raid English possessions in the West Indies during the second and third Anglo-Dutch Wars extended their raiding to the Chesapeake. During these assaults, a number of ships of the tobacco fleet were captured or burned, despite the presence of an English guardship.

Tobacco was loaded aboard ships bound for England in the spring.

Tobacco ships from England usually left their homeports in September and October, to avoid the hurricane season in the West Indies. Some would stop to stock up on supplies such as rum and citrus fruits. They would then continue on and arrive in the Chesapeake between October and January.

Once the ships arrived, they would call at a port of entry to obtain their clearance from the local authorities and pay any customs duties owed. Typically, cargo would include items ordered by planters and unconsigned goods, which would be announced for sale. Some of the wealthier planters would occasionally act as resident merchants and purchase large quantities of items and surpluses to be sold out of their homes or, in a few cases, out of a storehouse throughout the year. Depending on the accessibility of the waterways, either the ship or the ship's boat would sail from plantation to plantation, delivering consigned goods to the planter who had ordered them, engaging in trade or making arrangements for larger exchanges to take place. Some planters called at the ship to make additional purchases or deliver their tobacco.

Some planters called at the ship to make additional purchases or deliver their tobacco.

George Alsop, who immigrated to St. Mary's in 1658, wrote, "Between November and January there arrives in this Province Shipping to the number of twenty sail and upwards, all Merchant-men loaden with Commodities to Trafique and dispose of, trucking with the Planter for Silks, Hollands, Serges, and Broad-clothes, with other necessary goods . . ." Typically, those necessary goods included alcohol. In their written description of a trip through Maryland, two Dutch visitors noted that some planters would spend so much on spirits that they had little left to purchase the most needed items.

The Maryland colony benefited from the trade routes already developed by Virginia. Still, the process of exchanging goods could take a very long time, sometimes requiring several return trips to various plantations. Tobacco ships wintered in the Bay and left for England in the spring, while coastal trading ships operated most of the year.

Trade within the Colonies

I N THE EARLIEST YEARS OF SETTLEMENT, ENGLISH AND DUTCH vessels carried out what coastal trade there was, but it was not long before the colonies were building or buying ships to trade among themselves. New England, the other great English North American settlement of the 17th century, had no staple cash crop like tobacco, so its economy was based on shipbuilding and trade. By the mid-17th century, New England had established a thriving coastal and overseas trade network that included the Chesapeake. In contrast, the inhabitants of the Chesapeake owned few trading ships, despite their dependence on imported goods.

Shipbuilding, De Bry, 1594.

The Chesapeake colonies exported tobacco, corn (and by the 1680s wheat), pork, peas, hides (both tanned and raw), and a small number of furs to New England. Much of the tobacco was then re-exported to England or smuggled to Holland. From New England, the Chesapeake received salt cod and mackerel, timber (most likely milled timber since there was no shortage of wood in the Bay, but a severe shortage of mills to saw it), sugar, molasses, salt, earthenware, and re-exported English goods. Another major export to the Bay from New England was alcohol, both rum and wine from the Fayal and Madiera islands. Maryland and Virginia also sent corn and wheat, salt pork and beef, livestock, and timber for firewood and barrel staves to the West Indies and returned with sugar, molasses, rum, dyes, and fruits.

Included along with all the goods imported and transported by ship from other colonies, the Caribbean, England, and Europe would have been horses. In Maryland's early days the poor road system meant colonists covered more ground on foot or in small boats, so there were not many horses before the 1660s. But eventually Maryland must have become overrun with horses because laws were passed as early as 1671 restricting horses being brought in by land or sea from any "forraigne parts whatsoever." Despite the law, when the *Johns Adventure* left Boston for Maryland on May 5, 1688, thirty horses were included in her cargo.

In the 19th and 20th centuries, the Chesapeake became famous for oysters and crabs and products of the Chesapeake fishery were exported around the world. In the 17th and 18th centuries though, most of what was caught was used exclusively for local consumption. The residents of the Chesapeake enjoyed sheepshead, drum, sturgeon, crabs, and oysters, but the hot muggy summers made it difficult to salt or dry fish for export.

The colonists also traded with their American Indian neighbors, and ships brought items specifically for this purpose. Fur trading remained mostly in the hands of the Indians as Chesapeake planters were too busy with their tobacco crops to spend time hunting and trapping except as a means of putting additional food on the table. Trading with the colonists was one of the few ways American Indians had of obtaining the European goods they desired, the most popular of which were small axes, hatchets, hoes, sheets of copper, knives, combs of bone or horn, glass beads, jaw harps, hawk bells, scissors, linen shirts, wool blankets, and iron fish hooks. Shell beads, known as peake, roanoke or wampum, excess corn, and, occasionally, beans and peas were also marketable trade goods. The shell beads functioned as currency among the Indian peoples and could be used to trade for other commodities.

In early Maryland, licenses were required for foreigners to import or export goods within the borders of the colony. Foreigners included Englishmen from other colonies. Licensing was seen as a means of controlling the trade, ensuring that the governor got his cut and helping to prevent the sale of guns and ammunition to the American Indians. Unlicensed traders risked the confiscation of their ships if caught. In 1659, Daniel Hutt, a New England shipmaster, was accused of unlicensed trading and selling guns to the Indians. In his own defense, Hutt offered the rather weak statement that *". . . he hath not broken the Laws or Acts of this Province in so trading, as is alleged, And if any thing was committed by him in that kind, was through ignorance done, & not in contempt of the government or Laws of the Province."*

Needless to say, with such a defense, the court quickly found him guilty of illicit trade. The charge of selling guns was not proven, but the illegal trading conviction resulted in the confiscation of Hutt's ship. The conviction apparently did not discourage Hutt from trading in the Chesapeake, for a year later he reappears in the records as the master of a ship called *John's Adventure*.

The Slave Trade

NOT EVERYONE WHO ARRIVED IN THE COLONIES CAME willingly. On occasion people in England were kidnapped and sold into indentured servitude. The first people of African origin arrived at Jamestown in a Dutch ship in 1619. While slavery was practiced in the 17th-century Chesapeake, it did not initially form the primary basis for the labor force, especially in Maryland. One reason was economic: an indentured servant could be had for some eight to twelve hundred pounds of tobacco while a slave might cost five times as much. Newcomers, Europeans and African alike, suffered from "the seasoning," a series of illnesses that followed the seasons (hence the name). In the early 17th century, as many as one in three immigrants died of "the seasoning." If a servant died of the seasoning, a planter lost much less than he did if a slave died.

The changeover from indentured servants to enslaved labor occurred gradually, starting in the late 1600s. In the second half of the century, economic conditions in England improved while stories about harsh conditions and hard work in the colonies circulated. The number of those willing to take a chance as indentured servants diminished. Over time, the "seasoning" became less of a problem for both Europeans and Africans. With the decrease in the number of indentured servants available and the decreased likelihood of losing a slave to illness, the economic benefits of a slave became more attractive. While a slave might cost more, the slave was owned and worked for life rather than four to five years, and any children of the slave were also the property of the slave owner.

By 1670, the immigrant population of Virginia and Maryland was estimated to be 30,000, of whom only about 2,000 were of African descent. After 1680, the demand for slaves increased due to a rise in tobacco prices, but the Royal African Company, chartered by England in 1663 to carry out the slave trade, was unable to meet the demand. In 1685 the Royal African Company sent the ships *Speedwell* and *Two Friends* to Gambia to carry slaves to the Potomac and James rivers in what Arthur Middleton in *Tobacco Coast* describes as "half-hearted attempts" to supply the colonists' demands. It was not until 1698, when the trade was opened to all, that the numbers of slaves imported into the Chesapeake began to rise significantly. In Maryland, the African population rose from less than five thousand in 1704 to 25,000 in 1720, while in Virginia, the enslaved population rose from some 12,000 in 1708 to 30,000 by 1730. Thus, by the 1720s, the balance of the Chesapeake region workforce had switched from indentured servitude to enslaved labor. In the 17th century, slavery was already the primary source of labor on the English, French, and Dutch West Indian plantations and in the Spanish and Portuguese holdings in the New World, but for the Chesapeake, the horrors of the "Middle Passage" began to change the region forever during the 18th century.

Roll out the Barrel

The vast amount of goods moving in and out of the Chesapeake in the 17th century was typically contained in wooden casks, the cardboard box of the period. Casks came in a variety of shapes and sizes, ranging from the firkin, which held a mere nine gallons to the 36-gallon barrel up to the tun cask, which held 252 gallons.

The standard shipping cask for the carrying of tobacco was the hogshead. Although in liquid measure a hogshead generally held 64 gallons, in reality the size and weight of a tobacco hogshead varied widely in the 17th century. The primary reason for this was shipping costs. Shipmasters charged not by weight but by the number of hogsheads. Therefore it was in the interests of the planter to pack as much tobacco as possible into a hogshead, increasing the size of the hogshead if necessary. At various times, both Virginia and Maryland attempted to regulate the size of hogsheads, each trying to outdo the other in size. Maryland claimed it should be allowed a larger hogshead since its Oronoco tobacco was bulkier than the sweet-scented tobacco produced in Virginia. It was not until the 18th century that a measure of standardiza-

Casks, which came in several sizes, were the primary shipping container.

tion was achieved. By this time, the hogshead was 48 inches high and 32 inches wide and held upwards of half a ton of tobacco.

A cask has several advantages over other shipping containers. First, it is a great deal easier to move over short distances. Because of its shape, a cask may be turned on its side and rolled along a wharf with relative ease, no matter its weight. Even in tight spaces, casks are more maneuverable. Tilting it on its edge will allow it to be rolled through a narrow opening—as long as the opening is wider than the width of the cask. When it was absolutely necessary to move tobacco overland, large wooden hoops were affixed to the hogshead to prevent damage as the cask was rolled to the water's edge.

Moving cargo in the 17th century was a laborious enterprise

Another advantage of a cask is that, like a cardboard box, it can be taken apart when not in use. Broken down casks take up much less space and can be reassembled for use when needed. Cooperage, the art of making casks, was one of the few trades practiced in the early Chesapeake, and pipe staves, the strips of wood that form the sides of a barrel, were one of few non-tobacco exports from the Chesapeake.

The term "rolling road" came from the days when hogsheads of tobacco were rolled to ship landings.

Watery Highways

Tobacco can be grown in many areas of eastern North America, but the navigable waterways of the Chesapeake made shipping large quantities of tobacco to market easier and more profitable. It was possible for ships of considerable size to go nearly anywhere in the Bay or its tributaries, and smaller craft could reach almost any point unhindered. Although there are no rocks of any size in the Chesapeake, there are numerous shoals and sandbars so that the prudent shipmaster proceeded with some caution or brought aboard one of the few 17th-century pilots. One hazard that the first settlers found within the Bay, which no longer exists, was huge reefs of oysters, so large that a ship could run aground on them. As traffic on the waterways increased, the practice of dumping ballast into creeks and harbors threatened clear passage. As early as 1664, Maryland passed the first of several laws making it illegal for vessels to off-load ballast into harbors. Despite these and other hazards, most of the coastline of the Bay was accessible by boat.

The sheer physical labor involved in moving hundreds or even thousands of pounds of tobacco more than a few miles by land made water transport an attractive option. Overland movement of tobacco generally meant rolling a packed hogshead along the ground. This could be more or less difficult depending on the terrain and the size of the hogshead. The process could injure the tobacco if it was not tightly packed or if the hogshead incurred damage during its trip, a frequent occurrence. Water transport was easier, cheaper, and by far the preferred method.

The amount of effort involved to move objects by land and by water is easily calculated. Imagine a ship capable of loading 40 tons of cargo. A ship of this size could be handled by a crew of seven men, and with favorable winds it might cover 80 to 100 miles or more in a day's travel. On the other hand, moving 40 tons over land would require 60 to 80 wagons and each wagon would require at least two draft animals and a driver to manage them. Land transport would require a minimum of 60 wagons, 120 draft animals, 60 men, and a road. Because growing tobacco required large amounts of labor, a scarce item in the 17th-century Chesapeake, road building was not a high priority. Assuming a good road existed, this massive wagon train could move 10–15 miles in a single day. In wet weather, when the roads turned to axle-deep mud, movement slowed considerably! Contrary winds might hold the ship in port for days or even weeks, but wages for seven men are much less than wages for 60. No wonder then that water was the preferred method of travel.

In contrast to the Chesapeake region, the excellent tobacco country in northern North Carolina was very slow to develop because it has no deep-water harbors. Despite the great size of the Albemarle and Pamlico Sounds, they were too shallow to move anything but small vessels. Even after settlement in the late 17th and early 18th century, the inhabitants of northern North Carolina generally sent their products to the Chesapeake for shipment abroad.

In the colonial Chesapeake, cargo was not the only thing that traveled by water. Ships on the Bay also transported people. Ferries were a necessity for a land that was so cut by streams and rivers, and they were established early. The Maryland Assembly passed its first act regarding ferries in 1639, establishing a ferry across the St. George's River (as the St. Mary's River was called at the time). Ferries across Bretton Bay, the Wicomico, and other bodies of water followed. Ferry service was important enough for legislators to pass laws controlling the business. They prescribed conditions for operating a ferry, including fees and a schedule, and signals travelers would use to request passage. Legislation prohibited ferrymen from transporting anyone who might be fleeing indenture and mandated that horses and wheat be transported. Sometimes the government provided the boats to be used, paid the operator, and taxed citizens to support the ferry.

By the 18th century, a system of free public carriers existed side by side with private boats charging fees. Unlike the Virginia colony, years passed before Maryland attempted to regulate private ferries. Private ferries prevailed on the larger bodies of water while the free ferries supported by county levies tended to be on the smaller rivers, especially in the upper part of the Bay. Some ferries were free to all, some only free to county residents, but competition kept prices low. Many of the first roads in the tidewater region connected one ferry to another. The ferry at Whitehaven, Maryland, on the eastern shore of the Bay, is the oldest continuously operated ferry service in the United States, having provided transportation across the Wicomico River since 1683.

Below left, estimated size of a 50 ton vessel, like the Maryland Dove. *The ship on the right is a vessel of 400 tuns burthen, like the* Ark. *Drawings after Peter Egeli, 1973.*

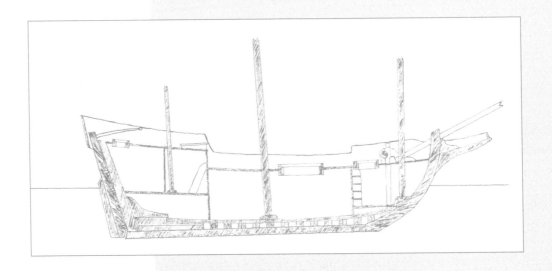

News of family, business, politics, scientific discoveries, and fashions of the day also arrived by ship as did personal letters, official documents, and gossip. Since many of the colonists could neither read nor write they often relied on visitors or crew to conduct correspondence for them. In 1695, official mail runs were begun in the Maryland colony. Several pick up points were established along the Potomac and Patuxent Rivers and linked to routes that ran from Williamsburg to Philadelphia.

Aside from practical considerations, families living along the water enjoyed the company of visitors that came by ship. A shipmaster was a popular dinner guest, entertained by the prominent families in the colony. Shipboard travelers were often the only contact the colonists had with home and the other colonies.

The tun, a measure of volume equal to 252 gallons, shouldn't be confused with the modern ton, a measure of weight equal to 2,000 pounds. In the 17th century, the tun was the measure of a ship's carrying capacity and ships were described in terms of tuns burthen. A tun of water, at 252 gallons, weighs close to a ton, or 2,000 pounds.

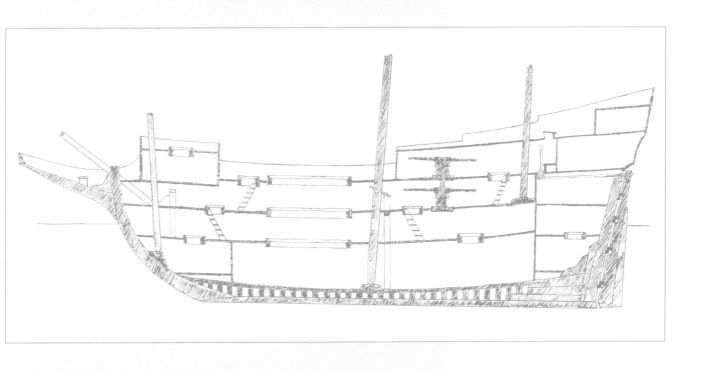

Getting Around

Sloop, Shallop, Pinnace, Ketch, Bark—These are some of the ship names used in the 17th century—sometimes to describe the same vessel! Today, sailing vessels are described by the type and configuration of sails carried as well as the number of masts. This practice began in the 17th century, but it appears that ships were more typically categorized by hull design and sometimes by the trade for which they were used.

Ships served the same functions as today's trucks, automobiles, and motorcycles. They were essential to carry out business, for communication, and to provide personal transportation. Eventually, pleasure boats appeared on the Bay. A variety of ship shapes and sizes evolved to serve these needs.

The fluyt, the truck of its time, would have been a frequent traveler on the Bay during the colonial period. The Dutch developed the fluyt at the end of the 16th century to carry a large cargo with a relatively small crew. Although they were slow and relatively defenseless, fluyts were used in great numbers because of these advantages. The English began copying the fluyt fairly quickly, but the building of English fluyts was actually banned by the English Admiralty out of fear that the lower crew requirements would lead to a lack of trained sailors to man the fleet in time of war. However, the continued conflicts between the English and the Dutch in the latter half of

Fig. 2

Fliste

A fluyt is characterized by its round stern and steep tumble-home, a ship shape that slopes inward from the waterline so that the deck is narrower in width than the hull below.

the 1600s led to a large number of captured Dutch fluyts being taken into English service.

Pinnaces are frequently mentioned in 17th-century sources and are one of the most loosely defined ship terms of the 17th century. The term was used to describe to everything from open pulling boats to large ocean-going vessels. Scholars note that "pinnace" is probably derived from the Latin word *pinus,* which means pine. It originally probably applied to vessels built of that wood, which were lighter than ones built of oak. By the 17th century, pinnace had become something of a catchall term and was often used to refer to a smaller vessel that accompanied a larger one on a voyage.

Ketches, barks, pinks, brigantines, and ships came in a wide variety of sizes, everything from 10 tuns burthen up to as large as 400 hundred tuns burthen. It would be tempting but incorrect to say that smaller vessels were used only within the Bay or for coastal trading and larger vessels were seagoing vessels. In the Boston Port Records of the late 17th century, there is a listing for the shallop *Anne* of 5 tuns burthen which departed Boston on 13 September 1687, bound for the Chesapeake carrying 5 hogsheads of molasses, a cask of wine, 2 casks of rum, provisions, salt and soap! The primary factor in any trading trip in the 17th century was profit. At times, large size could be a detriment. It would be much harder to fill a large vessel and the increased costs of maintenance and crewing could rapidly eat away an owner's profit margin. A larger vessel also increased the owner and shareholder risk and if the ship was lost the financial loss was much greater. In 1610, the English East India Company launched a vessel of 1,100 tuns called the *Trades Increase* at huge expense. On her maiden voyage in 1613, she was lost at sea, showing that size is no guarantee of safety at sea. Merchants preferred to follow the old policy of not putting all one's eggs into a single basket.

At 400 tuns burthen, the *Ark,* which carried the Maryland colonists and their belongings to their new home in 1634, was among the largest English merchant vessels of the time period. Port records show vessels as small as 10 tuns burthen regularly plying the coastline and even crossing the Atlantic.

A ketch is a flush-decked vessel (meaning they had no quarter deck) usually rigged with a mizzen and main masts.

In the 17th century, a brigantine was defined as a vessel with a square stern and a fore and main mast with square sails on the foremast.

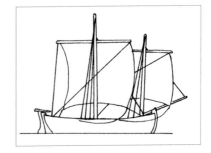

The word bark, *although sometimes used to refer to any vessel, was also a round sterned, two masted vessel with a single square sail on each mast.*

It was pleasant to hear them [the Yaocomaco] admiring everything, especially wondering, where in the world a tree had grown large enough to be carved into a ship of such huge size; for they supposed it had been cut out from a single trunk of a tree, like an Indian canoe. From Father Andrew White's *Chronicle of the Journey to Maryland.*

Bugeye. Courtesy of the Chesapeake Bay Maritime Museum.

In the early years, the vessels built in the colony were modeled after English or American Indian forms. Over time, the inhabitants of the Bay region developed their own unique craft for use within the waters of the Chesapeake Bay.

The English were quick to adopt the American Indian dugout for their own use. Dugouts were the equivalent of the family car. They couldn't carry much, but they served for short trips to visit neighbors, travel to the seat of government to do business, for fishing, or to carry tobacco from the plantation to the trade ship. Log canoes were popular in part because a basic canoe could be built by anybody with an axe. The English used iron tools when building log canoes, giving them a more familiar boat shape by pointing the ends. The ready availability of large logs and the scarcity of milled timber meant that in some areas the dugout survived well into the 20th century. The log canoe eventually evolved into one of the more distinctive and beautiful native sailing craft of the Chesapeake, the bugeye.

A step up from dugouts and often used for the same purposes were flats or scows made of pit sawn wood. Like dugouts, they were favored because people with little or no experience in boat building could put them together. These were flat-bottomed, blunt-ended craft designed to be poled, rowed, or, if the crossing was short, pulled across on a rope strung across the stream. These vessels were also sailed on occasion. Flats were more stable than dugouts and they could carry more, so they were very popular as ferries and as *lighters,* a boat that carries cargo from ship to shore and back. Although flats could handle rougher weather than dugouts, neither was particularly seaworthy, so their use tended to be restricted to sheltered waterways. If they ventured farther afield it would be on a relatively calm day.

Shallops were more seaworthy, or Bay-worthy, than dugouts or flats. The shallop was an undecked vessel ranging in length from around 15 feet to upwards of 30. Construction required the skills of an experienced shipwright, a scarce breed in the 17th-century Chesapeake. Shallops could be rowed or sailed. Eventually the shallop evolved into the sloop. Sloops were larger than shallops and fully decked with a single mast. Smaller sloops were used to run cargo and passengers up and down the Bay, while larger sloops were used in the coastal and even the trans-Atlantic trades.

A flat outfitted with a square sail.

While to modern ears the term barge implies something clumsy and unwieldy, the term was more loosely defined in the 17th century. The craft that Smith used to explore the Chesapeake was called a barge. It was probably simply a ship's boat or shallop that could be rowed or sailed as conditions warranted. A barge would have been on the large side for a ship's boat, capable of holding 15 men plus equipment and supplies. Most likely it would have been towed astern rather than carried on deck. The alternative was to break it down and stow it in pieces in a ship's hold. Such small craft were essential for exploration in unknown waters. When the water became shallow, they could be sent ahead carrying a man armed with a lead and line for sounding the depths and charting a safe

On the left, a shallop, with a pointed bow, is one of the true boat types that would be found in the Chesapeake. Also shown, two ships and log canoes.

course for larger vessels to follow. Within the Bay, such boats would be capable of very long voyages. They could go anywhere without fear of grounding on an unknown shoal, thus greatly extending the range of exploration.

The Maryland Assembly passed laws to encourage the growth of a local shipping industry. In 1661, the port duty was waived on vessels belonging to citizens of the colony. Slowly, a shipbuilding industry became concentrated on the eastern shore of the Bay. By the end of the 17th century there were 49 seagoing vessels in Calvert County and 26 in St. Mary's County. Manning the ships was not always easy though, as sailors who were dissatisfied with pay or conditions aboard a ship all too often deserted at the first opportunity.

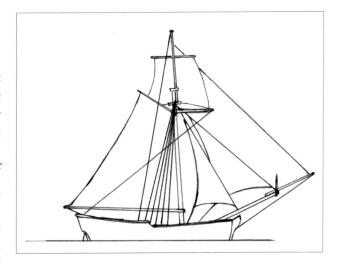

In the 1670s and 80s, a different type of vessel was seen in the Chesapeake region, in particular on the waters of the St. George's (St. Mary's), Potomac, and Wicocomico Rivers. It was the yacht of Charles Calvert, the third Lord Baltimore. King Charles II of England (1660–1685) popularized the idea of yachts and is often credited with originating the idea of yacht racing, but Lord Baltimore's yacht, the *Loyall Charles of Maryland,* may have been intended for a different purpose. In 1676, the captain of the *Loyall Charles* was told to display the proprietor's standard at the top of the masthead and was given permission to equip and arm the vessel to secure the province from invasion of ". . . any Robbers, Pyrates, Spies, or others that shall attempt any thing against this his Province . . ."

One hundred years after St. Mary's County was settled, roads had been developed and settlement was moving inland. Records show that the number of vehicles was twice the number of boats. These same probate records suggest an average person had two horses; the wealthiest individual in the sample also had two oxen.

With much travel done by water in the Chesapeake region, drownings were probably not uncommon. Operating a boat under the influence of too much drink was just as dangerous in 17th-century Maryland as it is today. In 1663, Daniel Clocker testified in court that he and another man, John Furnifeild, attempted to cross the St. George's (St. Mary's) river in a small canoe. They made the mistake of drinking far more than they should have before starting out. According to Clocker's testimony, ". . . the sd Furnifeild paddled the Canow, & betweene the Indian Pynt att West St Maries & the Church Poynt over agst it, the sd furnifeild fell out of the Canow & is now drowned & further sayth not."

The sloop evolved from the shallop. Although some sloops carried fore and aft spritsails, by the mid-17th century, almost all English sloops were gaff rigged.

Sailing Away from the 17th Century

CHANGE IN THE CHESAPEAKE CAME GRADUALLY AT FIRST, but with increasing speed as time went on. Tobacco prices underwent a slow but continual decline through the 17th and 18th centuries, marked by an occasional serious depression or recovery when the markets were glutted or bad harvests increased demand. When tobacco prices were very low, the residents of the Chesapeake turned to other crops. Typically, when prices rose again, the farmers returned to tobacco, but by the end of the 18th century, tobacco was no longer the sole cash crop. In the late 1700s, non-tobacco exports from the Chesapeake were worth about £120,000 a year and included wheat and bread, corn, peas, beans, pork and beef, pipe staves, lumber, and naval stores such as tar, pitch, and turpentine.

It wasn't until the mid-1800s that the Chesapeake became a major source of seafood for the United States and the world. Today, the Chesapeake is famous for oysters and crabs, and products of the Chesapeake fishery are exported around the world, but in the 17th and 18th centuries, most of what was caught was used exclusively for local consumption. The introduction of canning in the 19th century brought the Chesapeake fisheries into their own as a resource for exports.

In the 19th century, the Bay remained an important means of travel for the people who lived on and near its shores, but the sailing packets that carried passengers and freight up and down the Chesapeake were replaced by a faster and more reliable means of transport, the steamboat. Steamboat travel on the Bay started with a single route in 1813 and reached its height about 1906 when there were over 300 steamboat landings throughout the Chesapeake. In the summertime, steamers brought vacationers from the cities to resorts and amusement parks. For a while, Piney Point Maryland on the Potomac River enjoyed the name *Southern White House,* a place where the elite of Washington, including Presidents Monroe, Pierce, and Theodore Roosevelt, could escape the heat and humidity of the capital and enjoy the elegant hotel. However, the introduction of the automobile spelled the end of passenger transport on the Bay, and the Federal Highway Act sealed its fate. In the 1930s and 40s the number of steamships offering passenger service in the Bay dropped precipitously and by the 1950s only a few

The Anne Arundel *photographed by A. Aubrey Bodine
at Brome's Wharf in St. Mary's
City early in the 20th century.
©Jennifer B. Bodine*

excursion steamers were left in service. By the 1960s, these too had ceased operation.

Fleets no longer arrive from England each fall loaded with goods to trade for colonist's tobacco. Small trading ships no longer carry loads of salt cod, rum, sugar and other goods up and down the coast from New England to the West Indies. The modern highway system now carries both travelers and trucks around the Bay. Only a few islands rely on ferries to maintain contact with the world outside, and television and the Internet bring news into our homes.

Nonetheless, the Bay still serves as a highway. Each day freighters and tankers pass between the capes into the Chesapeake and destinations in Norfolk, Baltimore, and other ports. They are carrying not only goods but also oil to fuel the automobiles that have replaced the old steamers. In their wake, pleasure boats, both sail and power, cross the waters of the Bay. Watermen still ply their trade, fishing for crabs and oysters. Menhaden trawlers pull nets of their catch aboard.

Old buildings present their best face to the water, recalling a time when the "front" was on the river or Bay. But this can prove confusing to newcomers who expect "the front" to face the road and its modern-day traffic.

And once in a while, the watch-stander aboard a tanker or a yachtsman out for a cruise will catch sight of a small ship, odd-looking by modern standards, but possessing a unique beauty all the same, rigged with square sails, sailing the waters of the Bay. Representations of 17th-century sailing vessels, the *Maryland Dove* from Historic St. Mary's City, and the *Susan Constant, Godspeed,* and *Discovery* from Jamestown, still sail the waters of the Chesapeake, reminding modern eyes of the great Bay's long tradition as a watery highway.

Anderson, R.C. *The Rigging of Ships in the Days of the Spritsail Topsail.* New York. Dover Publications, 1994.

Baker, William A. *Colonial Vessels, Some 17th Century Ship Designs.* Barre, MA. Barre Publishing Co., 1962.

Baker, William Avery. *The Mayflower and Other Colonial Vessels.* London. Conway Maritime Press, 1983.

Baker, William Avery. *Sloops and Shallops.* Barre, MA. Barre Publishing Co., 1966.

Brewington, M.V. *Chesapeake Bay : A Pictorial Maritime History.* New York. Bonanza Press, 1956.

Brewington, M. V. *Chesapeake Bay Log Canoes and Bugeyes.* Cambridge, MD. Cornell Maritime Press, 1963.

Brewington, M. V. *Chesapeake Bay Sailing Craft.* Baltimore. Maryland Historical Society, 1966.

Davis, Ralph. *The Rise of the English Shipping Industry in the 17th and 18th Centuries.* Newton Abbot. David & Charles, 1972.

Gardiner, Robert. ed. *The Heyday of Sail the Merchant Sailing Ship 1650–1830.* Annapolis. Naval Institute Press, 1995.

Goldenberg, Joseph A. *Shipbuilding in Colonial America.* Charlottesville. University of Virginia Press, 1976.

Holly, David C. *Chesapeake Steamboats: Vanished Fleet.* Centreville, MD. Tidewater Publishers, 1994

Holly, David C. *Tidewater by Steamboat: A Saga of the Chesapeake.* Baltimore. Johns Hopkins University Press, 1991.

László, Veres and Richard Woodman. *The Story of Sail.* Annapolis. Naval Institute Press, 1999.

Middleton, Arthur Pierce. *Tobacco Coast: A Maritime History of the Chesapeake Bay in the Colonial Era.* Baltimore. The Johns Hopkins University Press, 1994.

Bibliography

Shomette, Donald. *Ghost Fleet of Mallows Bay and Other Tales of the Lost Chesapeake.* Centreville, MD. Tidewater Publishers, 1996.

Shomette, Donald. *Pirates on the Chesapeake: Being A True History of Pirates, Picaroons, and Raiders on Chesapeake Bay, 1610–1807.* Centreville, MD. Tidewater Publishers, 1985

Shomette, Donald. *Shipwrecks on the Chesapeake: Maritime Disasters on the Chesapeake Bay and Its Tributaries, 1608–1978.* Centreville, MD. Tidewater Publishers, 1982.

Wing, John F. *"Bound by God—for Merryland": The Voyage of the Constant Friendship, 1671–1672.* Annapolis. The Maryland State Archives, and the Maryland Historical Trust, 1999.